# Jazzin' Americana FOR TWO

## Early Intermediate to Intermediate Piano Duets That Celebrate American Jazz

### Wynn-Anne Rossi

Welcome to *Jazzin' Americana for Two*. This unique series is a journey through the jazz genre, honoring the history, diverse styles, and fabulous musicians who made this music great. While delving into appealing jazz styles, the performers will become familiar with the names of famous musicians like Chet Baker, McCoy Tyner, and Sarah Vaughan. From blues and bebop to boogie and rock, American jazz has made its profound mark on the music of the world.

Each duet is enhanced by interesting facts to awaken curiosity and broaden music education. Please encourage additional jazz listening and research as students navigate through the different styles. Rhythm workshops are included to help students count, then "feel" tricky jazz rhythms.

Please note that improvisation is not the focus of this series. Though improvisation is a key element in jazz, these books are designed as an introduction to the sounds of jazz. However, teachers and students may find it energizing to use a certain jazz style, left-hand pattern, or chord sequence as a springboard for free experimentation.

Enjoy this heartfelt, historic journey through *Jazzin' Americana for Two*!

## Contents

Alfred Music
P.O. Box 10003
Van Nuys, CA 91410-0003
**alfred.com**

ISBN-10: 1-4706-3983-1
ISBN-13: 978-1-4706-3983-9
Cover Illustration
Instrument Icons: © gettyimages.com / Leontura

# Struttin' Down Frenchmen Street

Music comes alive every evening on Frenchmen Street in the heart of the French Quarter of New Orleans. From *Dixieland* classics to new and experimental tunes, jazz captures memory and imagination at every corner.

Secondo

Wynn-Anne Rossi

## Rhythm Workshop

Tap rhythm 3x daily.

# Struttin' Down Frenchmen Street

Music comes alive every evening on Frenchmen Street in the heart of the French Quarter of New Orleans. From *Dixieland* classics to new and experimental tunes, jazz captures memory and imagination at every corner.

Primo

Wynn-Anne Rossi

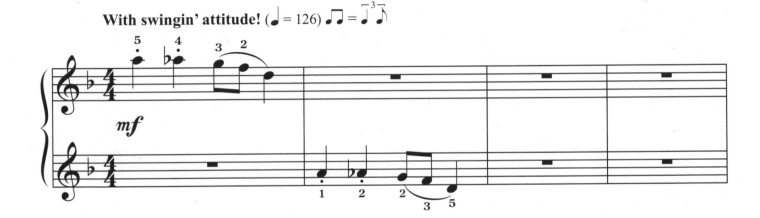

# Heartbreaker

Trumpeter Chesney Henry "Chet" Baker (1929–1988) lived a complicated life. After a street fight, he lost his front teeth and the ability to play his instrument. However, he conquered the challenge and eventually thrived in the *cool jazz* genre.

Secondo

Wynn-Anne Rossi

## Rhythm Workshop

Tap rhythm 3x daily.

mm. 7–8

# Heartbreaker

Trumpeter Chesney Henry "Chet" Baker (1929–1988) lived a complicated life. After a street fight, he lost his front teeth and the ability to play his instrument. However, he conquered the challenge and eventually thrived in the *cool jazz* genre.

Primo

Wynn-Anne Rossi

**Quietly expressive** ($\quarternote$ = 72)

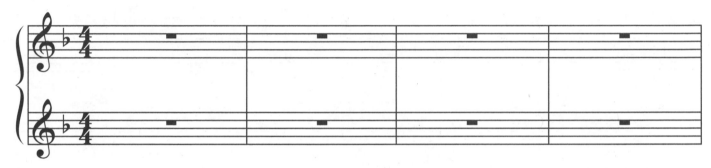

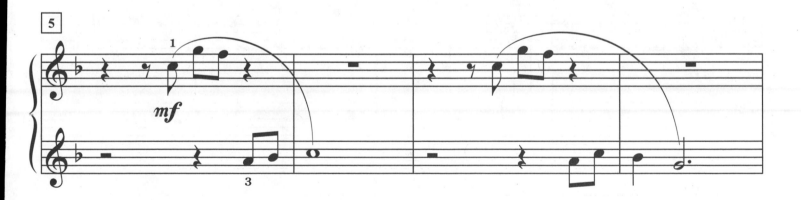

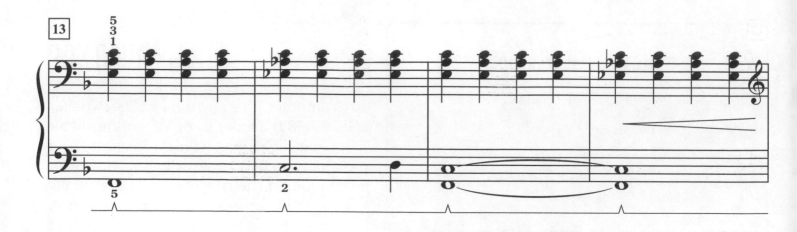

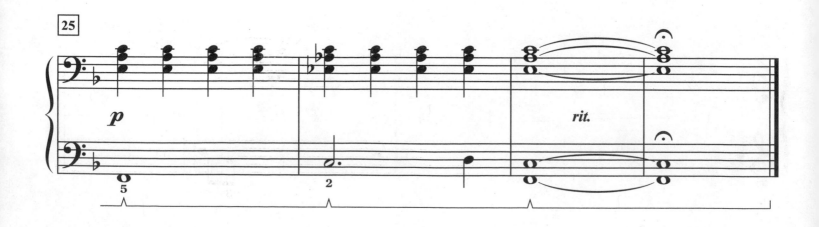

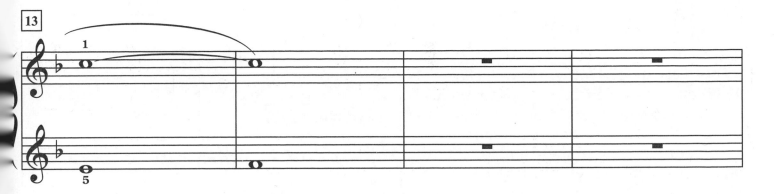

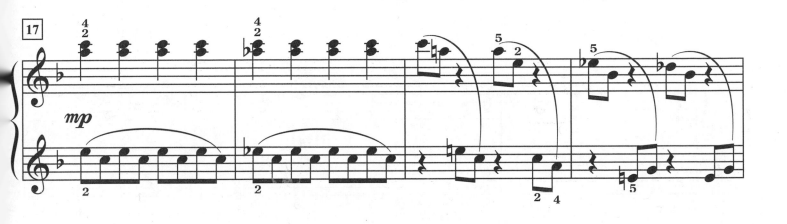

# Buddy Boobop

Pianist Earl Rudolph "Bud" Powell (1924–1966) excited audiences with his virtuosic style and unbridled expression. He helped pioneer the sound of *bebop*, a genre of jazz featuring fast tempos, complex chords, and unpredictable rhythms. Trumpeter Miles Davis (1926–1991) described Powell as "the greatest pianist in this era."

**Secondo**

Wynn-Anne Rossi

# Buddy Boobop

Pianist Earl Rudolph "Bud" Powell (1924–1966) excited audiences with his virtuosic style and unbridled expression. He helped pioneer the sound of *bebop*, a genre of jazz featuring fast tempos, complex chords, and unpredictable rhythms. Trumpeter Miles Davis (1926–1991) described Powell as "the greatest pianist in this era."

Primo

Wynn-Anne Rossi

# Waltz for Sarah

The rich, versatile voice of Sarah Lois Vaughan (1924–1990) could reach from a warm baritone range to high soprano. She had an impeccable sense of pitch and often referred to the "notes between the notes."

Secondo

Wynn-Anne Rossi

## Rhythm Workshop

Tap rhythm 3x daily.

# Waltz for Sarah

The rich, versatile voice of Sarah Lois Vaughan (1924–1990) could reach from a warm baritone range to high soprano. She had an impeccable sense of pitch and often referred to the "notes between the notes."

Primo

Wynn-Anne Rossi

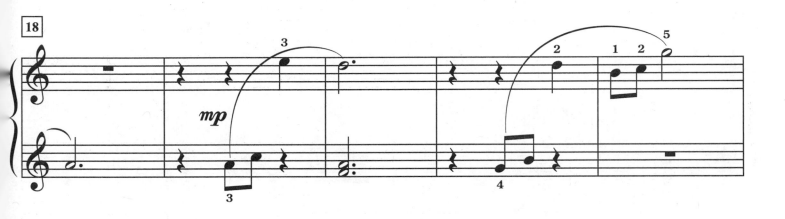

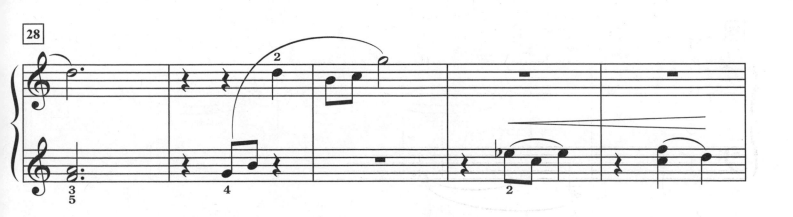

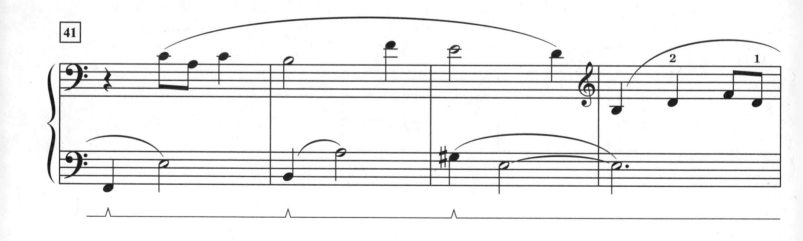

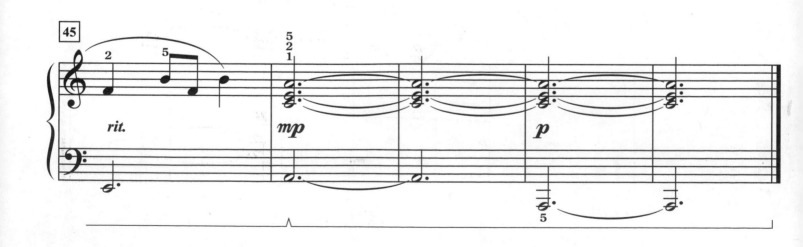

# Southpaw Spirit

Alfred "McCoy" Tyner (b. 1938) is one of the most energetic, influential jazz pianists of the modern era. Being a "southpaw" (person who is left-handed) contributes to his distinctive style, which features the lower bass range of the piano.

## Rhythm Workshop

Tap rhythm 3x daily.

mm. 9–10

Secondo

Wynn-Anne Rossi

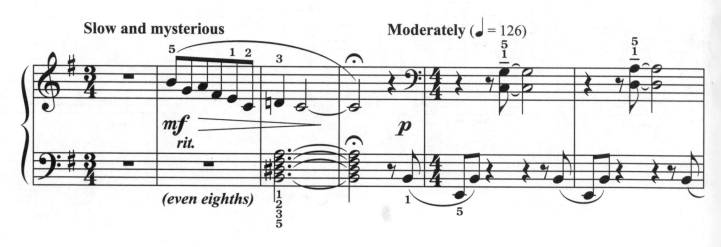

## Rhythm Workshop

Tap rhythm 3x daily.

mm. 15–17

# Southpaw Spirit

Alfred "McCoy" Tyner (b. 1938) is one of the most energetic, influential jazz pianists of the modern era. Being a "southpaw" (person who is left-handed) contributes to his distinctive style, which features the lower bass range of the piano.

Primo

Wynn-Anne Rossi

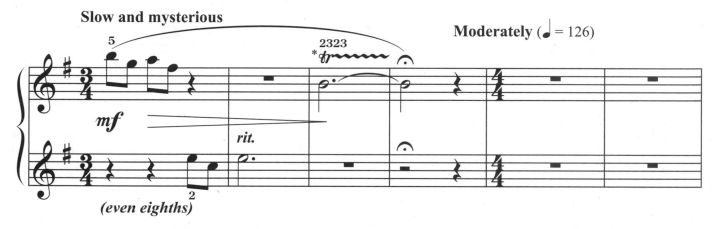

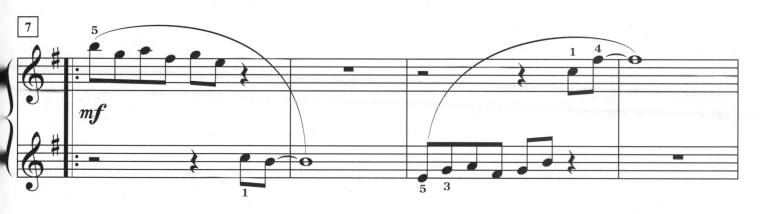

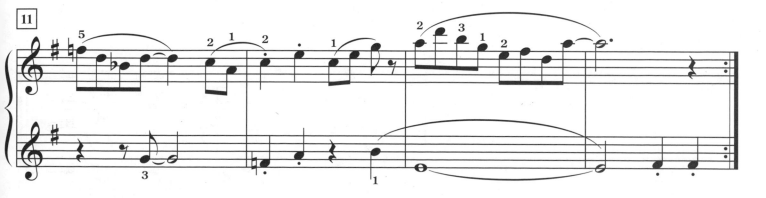

* Begin the trill on the main note.